From Vision To Venture To Victory

Great Is Thy Faithfulness

The History And Ministry Of
Northwest Independent Church Extension

From Vision
To Venture
To Victory

Great
Is Thy
Faithfulness

The History And Ministry Of
Northwest Independent Church Extension

Roy E. Sprague

WINEPRESS WP PUBLISHING

All Scripture quotations are from the King James Version of the Holy Bible.

ISBN 1-57921-132-1
Library of Congress Catalog Card Number: 98-60914

Vision to Venture to Victory

For the NICE 40th Anniversary

Bob Allen

Brent Olstad

Dedication

To all of the NICE missionaries who have faithfully
served their Lord. Their work, though often
unnoticed by the world, has been recorded forever
in the heart of God.

These are the heroes who, by their team effort,
have made possible that work which has been
accomplished through the
Northwest Independent Church Extension.

I salute you!

Stan and Virginia Poeschel

Bill and Sharilyn Peters

Acknowledgments

My deep appreciation to Noel Olsen, one of the founders of Northwest Independent Church Extension, who has provided wise leadership and faithful encouragement throughout the years.

My heartfelt thanks to Henry Boyd, the first director of the mission, who has modeled a vision for church planting and compassion for reaching souls.

My gratitude to Donald Strunk, the mission's second director, who demonstrated service with gladness and enthusiasm to venture.

My particular gratitude to Earl Brubaker and John Edgell for their support, ministry, and patience as assistant directors, serving with unique commitment to me and to the Lord.

My special thanks to Bill and Joy Cross, who provided such an ideal and beautiful place on Guemes Island, where in solitude this book was written. And especially to Bill, whose prayer and support for me has been unceasing.

To all those who have prayed for me while researching and writing, thank you.

To my wife, Elvia, all my love. Your assistance in editing has been invaluable. You have been a constant source of inspiration and support in the rewarding task of planting, establishing, and serving churches.

Noel and Lorraine Olsen, 1995

Earl and Shirley
Brubaker

Contents

Foreword

~~~

The Northwest Independent Church Extension (NICE) has been used of God to impact the northwestern states of our country. As an effective mission organization, it has become a role model for similar church extension ministries. Its formation and subsequent history as expressed in *From Vision to Venture to Victory* provide inspirational reading.

It is revealing to know how God led in many impressive ways prior to the organizational birth of this mission. After passing infancy and adolescence, now maturity has been reached. This is marked by its fortieth anniversary. Never deviating from its God given vision, the time has come for the mission's history to be written and the biblical principles upon which it is founded reiterated.

After many years as the mission's director, Roy Sprague is particularly suited to the task of writing this history. He grew up traveling with his parents in a ministry of evangelism and church planting. This heritage, coupled with his God-given abilities, has been used in a most significant way in the leadership of Northwest Independent Church Extension.

Having had a part in the ministry of NICE from its inception, it is a privilege to commend for your reading this record of God's faithfulness. You will sense in these pages not just facts and dates, but the dynamic spirit of motivation in the hearts and lives of those whom the Lord has used through these years.

It is my prayer that God will use this book to encourage many to serve with vision and venture for His glory.

DR. LOWELL C. WENDT

Preface

The purpose of this book is to recount the birth and the history of the Northwest Independent Church Extension. This ministry began in 1958 and throughout the ensuing years has witnessed the great faithfulness of God.

The birth of the mission was the result of *vision* by men of God. And that same vision is possessed by the NICE missionaries today. Many *ventures* of faith were made by God's servants throughout the years. These have resulted in people being saved, lives being changed, churches being planted, and communities being impacted for God's glory. Truly, the mission's commitment to the principles and patterns taught in the Scriptures have been honored by God in bringing blessing, growth, and *victory.*

In over 160 cities and towns, God has been pleased to use the NICE missionaries to plant, establish, and serve churches. When reviewing the history of the Northwest Independent Church Extension, there is one overriding observation; indeed, there is one underlying fact: "Great is Thy faithfulness!" An analysis of the past is of value only as we are challenged to "press on toward the mark for the prize of the high calling of God . . . " (Phil. 3:14).

Throughout this book, the account of spiritual victory is given primary focus. In forty years it has been abundant. However, the reader must keep in mind that in church extension ministry venture and victory are seldom realized without struggles, discouragement, and sometimes defeat. There are disappointments and hurts in ministry. Though these are not frequently stated in these pages, please know that they were often present. The advance of the gospel is a spiritual battle.

The ultimate victory is yet to be, when we stand before the throne of God and see "a great multitude . . . saying, Salvation to our God who sitteth upon the throne, and to the Lamb" (Rev. 7:9–10).

What a day that will be! Thank God that many will be before His throne because of the ministry of Northwest Independent Church Extension.

Part I

From Vision . . .

Vision
is sanctified imagination
that sees the things
that can be done
with God.

Chapter 1

The Embryonic Years

Where there is no vision, the people perish.
(Proverbs 29:18)

The minutes of the spring meeting of the Pacific Northwest regional of IFCA held at the Melrose Community Church of Roseburg, Oregon, March 17 and 18, 1958, state:

> President Wendt reviewed the IFCA position concerning our movement as a fellowship of independent churches, meeting for mutual prayer, study, fellowship, and voluntary cooperation in different fields. The local church remains independent, dependent upon God, and seeking to be conformed to the Scriptures. This makes it clear that it is the solemn duty of the regional to set up necessary machinery for local church extension. After questions, answers, and discussion concerning church extension, a motion was made by Ray Gustafson, second by Richard Schwab that the executive committee be empowered to draw up a proposed constitution, preliminary plans, and recommended procedure to carry out practical and necessary church extension in our regional. The motion carried, and

Elmer Wilder led in prayer, asking for God's direction and blessing.

It has often been stated this was the beginning of the Northwest Independent Church Extension. At the March 1998 IFCA regional conference, also held at the Melrose Community Church, this significant action was remembered. There were twelve people honored, who were also present in 1958. Thus began the mission's fortieth anniversary celebration.

In His Mind

But the beginning of NICE was long before 1958. What took place in 1958 was venture. What took place in 1958 was faith acting upon vision. And that vision began in the heart of God and was placed in the hearts of key men and women who were obedient to God's call.

When, in Matthew 16:18, our Lord Jesus said, "I will build My Church, and the gates of hell shall not prevail against it," the ministry of the Northwest Independent Church Extension was in His mind. The outreach of the gospel and the planting of churches through NICE was also in His heart when He said, "Go therefore and make disciples of all the nations, baptizing them in the name of the Father and of the Son and of the Holy Spirit, teaching them to observe all things that I have commanded you: and lo, I am with you alway, even to the end of the age" (Matt. 28:19–20).

Vision has been defined as "the ability to anticipate and make provision for future events; foresight; imagination; a vividly imagined thing, state, or occurance" (Webster's New International Dictionary). The obedience of God's servants to the Word of God, which resulted in the ministry of NICE, could accurately be called vision. Indeed, vision is sanctified imagination that sees the things that can be done with God.

Setting the Stage

Vision was required in 1943 when the Pacific Northwest regional of IFCA International was formed. It was not only the desire for fellowship, but also a concern for the outreach of the gospel on the part of the founders, which resulted in this significant development. These men were Ezra S. Gerig, Pastor of The Church of the Great Commission, Portland, Oregon; John Forsythe, Pastor of Gatewood Baptist Church in Seattle, Washington; and William Robertson, Pastor of The Metropolitan Tabernacle of Vancouver, BC, Canada.

In 1946, with a burden for souls, and belief that God could do great things, Wallace and Inez Wilson moved to Renton, Washington. They reached out to people with the love of Christ, and as a result they soon planted the Highlands Community Church. They began to envision that God could do that same thing in many other places. Dr. Wilson recently commented, "When you have something from the Lord that you know can be of help to others, you desire to share that in the most effective way possible."

Gordon and Lorraine Titus were obedient to God's call to move to Northern California in 1946. By faith, they saw the possibilities of what God could do in such places as Hornbrook, Happy Camp, Weed, Holmes Flat, and Fort Dick. They began Bible classes and made contacts with people for the purpose of gospel outreach.

Knowing that God was working, the Tituses appealed to their home church for help. In 1947, their pastor, Lowell Wendt, and their Sunday school superintendent, Henry Boyd, responded by coming to Northern California with a team of workers. This team from Montecito Park Union Church and BIOLA University (at that time it was only a college) went to place after place with the message of the love of Christ.

That same summer of 1947, the Tituses, together with that team of workers, conducted a Bible camp at Mt. Lassen National Park. The speaker was Dr. Lowell Wendt, who faithfully taught the Word morning and evening. On Friday night the message was from Romans 12:1–2, where Paul urges, "I beseech you therefore . . . that you present your bodies a living sacrifice, holy, acceptable unto God, which is your reasonable service. And do not be conformed to this world, but be transformed . . . that you may prove what is that good and acceptable and perfect will of God."

Dr. Wendt challenged the young people concerning God's desire that they present themselves as a living sacrifice for His use. When the invitation was given, along with many others a thirteen year old boy stepped forward to present himself to the Lord for His service. That boy was Roy Sprague. I'll never forget that day, nor have I forgotten God's call upon my life.

In 1948, because of their personal observation of the spiritual need of the Northwest the year before, Henry and Margaret Boyd spent the summer in Northern California conducting vacation Bible schools and reaching out to people with the gospel. One of the communities they visited was Fort Dick.

God Moves His People

Noel Olsen was a young man with a great desire to preach the Word and to spread the gospel. In 1948, following graduation from Multnomah School of the Bible, Noel accepted the pastorate of the North Bonneville Community Church. After his marriage to Lorraine Denney, they faithfully served the church together. They also began to have an increasing burden for many spiritually unreached communities.

As a result of that concern, and by the request of Lorraine's brothers, Noel and Lorraine moved to the Crescent City area of Northern California. Noel worked for the Denney Brothers Logging Company and began a home Bible class. As God blessed, people were saved and believers began to grow.

Because of their contact with the small Sunday school at Fort Dick, both Gordon Titus and Henry Boyd urged Harry and Selma Sprague, who traveled in Needy Place Evangelism, to come to Fort Dick to conduct a series of evangelistic meetings. Thus in the fall of 1949, the Spragues came to Fort Dick. Roy was asked by his Dad to lead the singing in the meetings. What an opportunity for a fifteen year old boy, but what a challenge as well. Through that, I realized that, my life and my actions must square with my words.

God blessed through these meetings; people came to Christ, and believers continued to grow. One night, two young couples, Jack and Joyce Perry and Bert and Alice Rhodus, came to the meetings. My dad noting their enthusiasm for the Word of God asked about their relationship to Christ. Jack said, "Yes, I'm saved; and I'd like you to meet the teacher of our Bible class, Noel Olsen." So it was planned that Roy and Harry Sprague would meet and talk with Noel Olsen.

But the next day when we went to the Craig Lumber Company and asked a Mr. Olson if he was a Bible teacher, he answered, "I don't teach the [blankety-blank] Bible!" As we left, I can remember my Dad saying, "That must have been the wrong man." But we persisted, and the next day went to the Denney Brothers Logging Company. This time we met, not Mr. Olson, but Mr. Olsen! We talked to him about the things of the Lord. He came to the meetings at Fort Dick. It wasn't long before he became the founding pastor of the Fort Dick Bible Church.

Common Threads

Through the years of his ministry at Fort Dick, there were many who came to Christ. The church was organized and grew numerically and spiritually. In fact, the church attendance exceeded the population of the town! With this growth came an increasing burden to reach out to nearby communities with the gospel. As a result, Bible classes and a Sunday school began in the community of Gasquet. Soon the Gasquet Bible Church was organized.

By this time, Henry and Margaret Boyd sold their business in the Los Angeles area and in obedience to the Lord's guidance moved north for ministry. Henry recently stated, "We had a vision and burden for getting the gospel message to the unreached areas of the Pacific Northwest. God called me to ministry in 1935, and I've seen much of the fulfillment of that call with NICE. You know the starting of churches is a pioneer ministry, and we need more people to get this vision and reach out to needy areas."

Not long ago, reflecting on that time, Noel commented, "Henry and Margaret Boyd came to help us in our Gasquet project. God gave both Henry and me a great desire to plant new churches. We believed that God could multiply this vision into dozens of Bible churches in the Northwest." Under Noel's leadership, similar efforts were made by the Fort Dick Bible Church to reach out with the gospel and plant churches in Brookings, Oregon and Klamath, California. "We began to look for other men who had the same burden and desire for planting churches," Noel stated.

In 1953, Richard and Eleanor Schwab came to serve the Burke Avenue Chapel in Seattle, Washington. The emphasis of their ministry was a strong commitment to teach the Word of God and to reach out to people.

In 1954, Lowell and Marie Wendt moved to Tacoma, Washington to serve the Lake City Community Church. "We knew in making this move that the Pacific Northwest was one of the least churched areas of the country, and thus one of the most spiritually needy; we believed that God might be pleased to use us," observed Dr. Wendt in reflecting on this time. Thus by 1958, he was serving as the president of the Pacific Northwest regional of IFCA.

In response to God's direction, Charles and Marge Lyman came to the Dieringer Bible Church in 1956 to develop a Bible centered ministry with a decided emphasis on outreach and missions.

The common threads for each of God's servants is obvious—vision, obedience, burden for souls, commitment to planting churches.

Therefore, it was not by chance that at the IFCA regional conference at the Melrose Community Church in

March 1958 the following people were in attendance: Elmer Wilder, Wallace Wilson, Gordon Titus, Richard Schwab, Charles Lyman, Lowell Wendt, Henry Boyd, and Noel Olsen. They were there not only for fellowship, but also they came because of a mutual burden to do a work for the glory of God. They were divinely brought together with the commonality of great vision, great burden, and great trust in a great God!

Thus, when the minutes of the 1958 meeting record "It is clear that it is the solemn duty of the regional to set up necessary machinery for local church extension," we emphatically ask, "How could they have done anything else!"

The Northwest Independent Church Extension began in the heart of God. As we understand His heart and relinquish our own desires, we become ready to venture for His glory. As we become intimately acquainted with the character of God, we know we can trust Him to be all-sufficient.

On March 18, 1958 some great and exciting ventures began for His glory. "I don't believe any of us envisioned NICE as we now see it. The mission's outreach and influence has literally covered the United States," stated Charles Lyman. Richard Schwab echoed, "What God has wrought!"

Vision which comes from God will always result in ventures of faith!

Henry and Margaret Boyd, 1958

Noel and Lorraine Olsen,
and Family, 1963

Yes, Lord!

I was not disobedient to the heavenly vision
(Acts 26:19)

Vision to believe God was the constant challenge before the founders of the mission. Rev. Richard Schwab, the first secretary of the board, expressed this when he said, "The mission needs to keep on dreaming! Dreaming in the sense of scripturally 'lengthening the cords and strengthening the stakes.' To realistically face the challenge of God's will for the mission is not optional, but imperative to 'keep on going on' until He comes. Let us never be satisfied—greater prayer, greater support, greater praise, and greater outreach! May God grant it!"

From its beginning, the purpose of the mission has been the planting and development of Bible believing churches. The mission ministry was confined to the states of Washington and Oregon at its inception, expanding to part of Northern California in 1960, to Idaho in 1965, and to Nevada in 1975. By request of the Montana IFCA regional, its ministry was extended to Montana in 1977.

These steps of faith were approved by the board of directors. Yet, those serving in this capacity in 1965 were different men than those elected by the regional to serve in 1975 or 1977. God has graciously provided board members since 1958 who are men of faith and godly vision.

Obedience Emulated

Commitment to obedience has been the pattern followed by NICE church planters, missionary pastors, and leaders. Truly, it has been honored by the Lord.

When Henry Boyd accepted the call of the new mission to serve as the director in 1958, it was the result of great faith. There was no certain salary offered. This same commitment was demonstrated by Henry and Margaret when they moved to Loomis, Washington to pioneer the Loomis Community Church, and to Sauvies Island, to Chelan, to North Bend, to Skykomish, to Winnemucca, to Cave Junction, to Susanville, to Deer Park, and to Astoria. In fact, it only takes a brief visit with Henry today (age 94) to observe that he still possesses great vision and trust in our great God!

Trust in God was primary when Don Martin came to pioneer the churches at Carlton, Mazama, and North River, Washington, and at Council and Deary, Idaho. In fact, through the ministry of Don and Carol there are today nineteen different Christian workers serving the Lord in fields of ministry throughout the world.

It was vision and faith that caused Don and Joanne Strunk to accept the call to serve the Keyport Bible Church in 1959. It took even greater confidence when Don, with Joanne concurring, agreed to become the second director in 1962, because there was still no promise of a certain salary. That would require that Don not only serve as the mission's director, but also that he pastor a church. For a time, he also operated the family dairy farm. During Don's years as the mission director, the mission grew in its outreach and ministry, and the number of missionaries increased to twenty-one. Vision was also a factor when the Strunks moved to Idaho to serve the Cambridge Bible Church and to Manzanita, Oregon to serve the Calvary Bible Church.

When Roy and Elvia Sprague began to serve as the mission's evangelist in 1960, they were aware of several things:

1. God was calling them
2. God would meet their needs
3. God would open the doors to places of ministry
4. God's Word was needed in the Northwest

From 1960 through 1963, they traveled with their family to over 130 different cities and towns. During this time, God used His Word to draw over 1100 people to faith in Christ!

In 1970 the Spragues were asked by the board of directors to serve as the mission's director. The primary factor in saying yes was their faith, for the matter of salary was still, no certain salary. The total income to the mission's general fund averaged just under two-hundred and fifty dollars per month. This would have to be God's doing, or it would never be possible.

Gordon and Lorraine Titus claimed God's promises that He would supply their needs when they moved to Sequim, Washington to begin the Sequim Bible Church.

Today, the church is a congregation of over 500 people, with great involvement in worldwide missions.

Following twelve years of ministry in Washington and Oregon, Jerry and Lois James moved to Alabama to begin the Gulf Region Association for Church Extension. Vision was involved in this step of faith for new churches.

The wind was a factor in bringing John and Jane Edgell to serve with NICE in 1974. While walking down the hall of the Appalachian Bible College, the wind came though an open window and blew a leaflet from the table to the floor at John's feet. He looked at it and read, "Since you're special, why not be NICE?" This was the initial factor God used to bring them to Washington, where He used them to revive a sick church. Today John serves as the mission's assistant director, helping, encouraging, and serving the missionaries and the churches.

Vince and Brenda Ortiz moved to Oak Harbor, Washington in 1974 not knowing one person who lived in town. They did know that God was leading. They planted the Family Bible Church, which today is a growing, dynamic ministry of 700 people with a worldwide outreach.

Obedience to the Lord was evident on the part of Garland and Roberta Shinn as they left a successful pastorate in 1975, to come to Reno, Nevada. As a result, they not only began the Faith Bible Church in Reno, but also were used to start or help develop eleven other churches.

A small church needed help; yes, they would be willing to go, answered Bill and Mildred Cross. God blessed and the Faith Baptist Church of Florence, Oregon grew. Bill later became NICE's administrative assistant. Again, obedience to the Lord.

Agreeing to come to Calvary Bible Church of Carson City, Nevada for two weeks, Charles and Alice Holgate stayed in Nevada for seven years. During that time they were used of God to pioneer five new churches and to lead many people to Christ.

When Earl and Shirley Brubaker resigned the pastorate of Community Bible Church of Cave Junction, Oregon to move to the Bend/Redmond area, they knew it would be a challenge. They ministered to over 325 people one Sunday and to eight the next. Of these, five were their own family. But it was God who called them, and the Independent Bible Church began and was used to reach many families. It was also an act of faith when the Brubakers accepted the call of the mission to serve as assistant director in 1988.

The phone rang, and Keith and Marnella Lyons asked if there was a place they could be used where no one else would go. God led them to Round Mountain, Nevada and then to Pahrump, Nevada. This last year they have been used of God to bring several men and women, as well as over 100 children to the Savior.

Never was vision more obvious, nor faith more evident than when the Sunset Bible Church and its elders Lyle Nichols, Ray George, and W. D. Page offered half an acre of property to the mission, to build a headquarters building. And again Bill Cross said, "Yes, I'll be willing to supervise the construction." Together, with Jack Clapp, Maco Allason, Wayne Stewart, and a host of volunteers this beautiful building of 4,300 square feet was built. God's supply was demonstrated in miraculous ways. There were many volunteer workers and hundreds of financial supporters, which allowed the building to be completed totally debt free!

Men and Women of Faith

This reads like a twentieth century version of Hebrews 11. And, indeed, it is. All of these, and more, were men and women of faith. As Hebrews 11:32 states, "What more shall I say, for time would fail me to tell of . . . "

Don and Jody Wantland moving to Acme, Washington and seeing six men come to Christ that first year.

Jim and Kathy Miller approaching a man with gun in hand and later leading him to Christ, as well as almost thirty others as the Baker Bible Church was founded.

Dan and Nancy Wentworth coming to the Dayton/Dundee, Oregon area not knowing anyone, but trusting God to use them. In the first six weeks nineteen people trusted Christ and Crossroads Bible Church began.

Steve and Celeste DeFord traveling across the country from Maryland to Columbus, Montana, where many people responded to the Word of God.

Prentice and Louree Boyd pioneering a ministry in Mt. Angel, Oregon—a town which is 92 percent Roman Catholic. Praise God, He has changed lives there.

Andy and Cheryl Simonson starting the Quilcene Bible Church, where over a dozen people came to Christ the first year, and now a new building is being completed.

Jeff and Mary Mullins beginning a new church in their home at Rainier, Oregon. Most of the members are new converts and what a hunger they have for God's Word!

Bob and Judi Allen being instrumental in planting two churches in Belgium, and then accepting the call to serve as NICE's director of ethnic ministry. What God has done! . . .

Jesùs and Maria Cordova saying, "If God is calling us, we cannot do anything else but obey." Thus, they moved to Yakima, Washington, where God has honored their vision with two churches starting and several hundred people coming to Christ.

There's Jerry and Laura Conklin, Kelley and Michelle McCormick, Frank and Wendy Emrich, Larry and Linda Ott, Bill and Sharilyn Peters, and . . . and "These all, having obtained a good testimony through faith . . . " (Heb. 11:39).

Saying yes may cost—but always it pays! For God truly honors obedience. He does not anoint methods; He anoints men and women to do a job for Him.

School of Ministry Graduates, 1991

Part II

. . . to Venture . . .

Wallace and Inez Wilson—
Noel and Lorraine Olsen, 1963

Board Retreat, 1963
Harrah, Strunk, Schwab, Lyman, Boyd

Chapter 3

The Birth of a Mission

The members of the Pacific Northwest regional of IFCA International voted unanimously "that the executive committee be empowered to draw up a proposed constitution, preliminary plans and recommended procedure to carry on practical and necessary church extension in our regional." This vote took place on March 17, 1958.

The executive committee lost no time in carrying out the action initiated in March. On April 8, 1958, Wallace Wilson, Mcrold Westphal, Lowell Wendt, Charles Lyman, and Henry Boyd met at the Highlands Community Church of Renton. They made the following recommendations:

- A church extension organization be incorporated for the Pacific Northwest
- The name be Northwest Independent Church Extension or New Independent Church Extension, either name allowing the acronym NICE
- The constitution draft be formed within the next two months

- Mr. W.H. Boyd be appointed as the director
- These matters be ratified at the fall regional
- Churches and Sunday schools get behind this program immediately in prayer and financial support

The next regional conference was hosted by the Burke Avenue Chapel of Seattle on October 20 and 21, 1958. The minutes record "that Henry Boyd gave an excellent report on the mission project. He illustrated with a map the places where there is great need of churches. His financial report was a conscience-stinger, as we have not been helping our director financially."

Various men of the regional gave suggestions and spoke concerning the need of this ministry. "A motion was made by Russell Peet and seconded by Dan Sauerwein that the recommendations made by the regional executive committee be adopted, with the name 'Northwest Independent Church Extension' chosen, and that Lyman, Wilson, Schwab, Olsen and Boyd be appointed as the board of directors." This motion was carried unanimously.

Spiritual Needs were Primary

On November 28, 1958, the first meeting of the appointed board of directors was held at the Navy Yard City Bible Church in Bremerton, Washington. As with any new mission, organizational matters were discussed. Olsen was appointed to draft a constitution, Wilson to investigate the legal steps for incorporation, and Schwab to inquire about the IRS regulations.

But the need for churches and the spiritual needs of people were too urgent to wait for organization. Director Henry Boyd, with his wife, Margaret, was busy and involved in gospel outreach at Mount Vernon, Oregon. In their November prayer letter, they wrote, "What a tremendous blessing the Lord brought us—sixty in Sunday school! One lady brought eighteen children, and for all of them this was the first time they had attended a Sunday school. What a privilege is ours to open the Word of God to them. Pray with us that the love and compassion of Christ may so fill our hearts that many of these boys and girls may soon be won for Him. There are also two adults who are very near to salvation."

They were also involved in building a parsonage at Mount Vernon, as well as doing survey work throughout Oregon and Washington. In addition, they made contacts with churches and schools for workers.

On January 30, 1959, the board of directors of the mission met at Highlands Community Church in Renton, where it was moved "that Northwest Independent Church Extension be incorporated with a seven man board." At this meeting, board officers were elected as follows:

- Noel Olsen, President
- Wallace Wilson, Vice President
- Richard Schwab, Secretary
- Charles Lyman, Treasurer
- Henry Boyd, Mission Director

The brethren spent much time "in examination, clarification, and revision of the draft of the mission's constitution."

At the spring conference of the Pacific Northwest regional of IFCA, meeting at Multnomah School of the Bible in Portland, the proposed constitution and elected board members were approved by the regional members. It was expressed that "there must be a close working relationship between the regional and NICE, yet the mission must be free to carry out functional decisions. To assure this, two basic checks would be: (1) Elected members of the board of NICE or their removal is determined by the regional; and (2) The Doctrinal Statement of NICE must be the same as that of the IFCA."

At this same meeting, Mr. Joseph Kempston of Tacoma and Mr. William H. Denney of Reno were approved as two additional members of the board of directors.

Missionaries Were Accepted

One of the first workers to be accepted by the mission was Marie Brown, who served at Bates, Oregon. She began ministry there even before the mission was fully organized. Board secretary Richard Schwab wrote, "Before the basic work of organization has been laid for the mission, the Lord has opened fields, allowed splendid contacts with needy congregations, and brought contacts with and applications from mission workers. For this we thank the Lord and in it see His leading to venture on by faith."

During these formative days, the board of directors met every month to handle the necessary organization and business at hand. On May 20, 1959 "the applications of Gordon and Lorraine Titus were approved to serve as workers under the auspices of NICE."

The board, at their August 4 meeting in Bremerton, discussed and approved:

- The articles of incorporation
- The mission workers agreement
- The church-mission policy

With praise to God, Henry Boyd reported in his August letter "that seventeen children were dealt with who accepted the Lord during VBS at Mt. Vernon, Oregon. Immediately following the Bible school we began a week of evangelistic meetings with Troy Costlow of Los Angeles. The Lord was very gracious and souls were saved. At present we are in Tacoma and are helping a group of believers start a church in Skyway."

It was reported at the October 5 meeting that "the Articles of Incorporation had been sent to all the board for their signatures and has now been submitted to Olympia for filing."

The minutes also state that "Olsen brought a challenging report of the survey trip which he and Henry Boyd made to Carlton and Loomis, Washington. Certain churches needing pastors were discussed." The mission application form was drafted and printed, as well as attractive letterhead paper and envelopes. A corporate seal was ordered and promotional literature designed and printed.

During this period of birth, with all of the meetings necessary to establish proper organization, the brethren continued to venture on by faith to do the work God had called—a work of planting churches and serving God's people.

This commitment to servant leadership has continued throughout the years of ministry. The mission's theme verse is indeed the foundation:

For we preach not ourselves, but Christ Jesus the Lord, and ourselves your servants for Jesus' sake. (2 Cor. 4:5)

Praise God for the First Year

The October 1959 IFCA regional convened at the Highlands Community Church of Renton. There was interest in the work of NICE by all, including the ladies, so much so in fact that the minutes state, "A murmuring in the mulberry trees led to our invitation to the women to stay with the men for the report and business session of NICE."

President Olsen gave praise to God for the completion and approval of the incorporation papers for the mission. "In fact," he said, "Pastor Wilson received a phone call just this morning during the prayer service that the papers had been received and were approved by the State of Washington."

All present received copies of the constitution, congregation statement of policy and mission worker statement of policy.

With gratitude to God, Director Henry Boyd reported the following appointments or placements during the mission's first year:

- Rev. Don Martin–Carlton, Washington
- Rev. and Mrs. Ed Snyder–Loomis, Washington
- Mr. and Mrs. Henry Boyd–Mt. Vernon, Oregon
- Mr. and Mrs. Don Strunk–Keyport, Washington
- Rev. and Mrs. Gordon Titus–Gasquet, California

- Rev. and Mrs. Gene Almquist–Mt. Vernon, Oregon
- Rev. and Mrs. Charles Witcher–Hillsboro, Oregon

Those present were challenged by Charles Lyman and Wallace Wilson concerning the promotion of NICE, "that pastors and churches ask the Lord what they should do to speed the Lord's moving in fields of ministry, churches, and people through the mission."

The meeting concluded with President Olsen asking that all stand, and then he said, "Let's praise the Lord for His goodness during this first year! Let's pray that NICE may be Holy Spirit empowered to the salvation and edifying of many souls, and to the glory of God!"

Don and Carol Martin, James and David: 1970

Richard Schwab

Chapter 4

On the Grow

The direction and provision of God continued to be evident to all those serving with NICE. Several churches included the mission in their missionary giving, but the total income, in all accounts, for November 1959 was $272. Truly this was a venture of faith!

The good hand of God was evident in the encouraging response of Christian leaders from throughout the country, indicating their willingness to serve on the board of reference. These were:

- Rev. B.A. Adams–California
- Dr. Roger J. Andrus–Missouri
- Rev. James Braga–Oregon
- Dr. Don Hillis–Illinois
- Mr. Kenneth Taylor–Illinois
- Dr. John F. Walvoord–Texas
- Dr. Lowell C. Wendt–California

President Olsen reported to the board in February 1960 that he had been invited by the executive secretary of IFCA to represent NICE at the IFCA national convention. With enthusiasm, he indicated "that a five foot by twelve foot mural painting was being made, featuring Mt.

Rainier, Multnomah Falls, a 707 jet, and the Washington coastline," and that he and Mrs. Olsen planned to be present.

The mission leadership secured a bid to print a two-color brochure at forty dollars per thousand. This seemed in line, so 2,000 were ordered.

Promotion and Reporting

At the IFCA regional conference in March 1960, Director Henry Boyd reported "that a letter regarding NICE had been sent to every graduating senior at Multnomah School of the Bible, Briercrest Bible Institute, Moody Bible Institute and Grand Rapids School of the Bible and Music."

At this same meeting, held at Evergreen Bible Church in Vancouver, the missionaries were introduced, and each gave a report of their ministry. Prayer was requested concerning applications received from Roy and Elvia Sprague, a young California pastor and his wife willing to serve as mission evangelist.

"The Lord added to the Church five souls last Sunday—one man and four juniors," wrote Henry Boyd to the board in June 1960. And Margaret added, "Did you ever say 'it can't be done?' Of course you have, and so did we; but again the Lord has showed us that 'with God all things are possible.' But who would have imagined Henry leading a choir, but he did!"

At the August meeting, reports were received concerning the work God was doing at each of the mission points and of a new ministry beginning at Jacksonville, Oregon by Gordon and Lorraine Titus.

In October inquiries were received for ministry from churches in Hansville and Birch Bay, Washington and

Roy and Henrietta Rhodes were accepted as missionaries. The board was also corresponding with the IRS for necessary tax exemption.

As 1960 came to a close, Henry Boyd, mission director, gave an encouraging review to the board. He reported, "It would seem that the Lord has given us some fine missionaries who have the vision and initiative to move out and start other works."

Many new opportunities came in 1961, as well as discussion and clarification of the director's ministry. The blessings of God were evident at Loomis, where Henry and Margaret Boyd were serving, but there were many other areas of need—how do we meet them all?

Changes in Leadership

The board met at the Dieringer Bible Church of Sumner on May 26, 1961, to draft a job description for the director's ministry. At this same meeting, Robert Archer was examined for ordination to the gospel ministry.

The October 1962 meeting of the IFCA regional was held at Grace Haven Lodge at Cannon Beach, Oregon. During this meeting it was suggested that an annual NICE Sunday be scheduled in as many regional churches as possible. The minutes record that "it was moved by Wilson and seconded by Boyd and unanimously carried that NICE make application to the IFCA as a church extension organization."

The missionaries continued to serve faithfully and to venture into new areas of ministry. But at the IFCA regional conference hosted by the Community Bible Church of Cave Junction in March 1962, there were changes for the mission as Henry Boyd "recommended to the board that in view of his relationship to the Loomis project, and in view of his lack of physical stamina and ability to travel, that the board seek another director within the year, and the board consider Reverend Donald Strunk as the man to be trained for this ministry, and that the Boyds continue their work at Loomis as NICE missionaries."

President Olsen reported that Donald Strunk consented to serve as assistant director for one year while training to become the director. He also mentioned the Strunk's finances and urged each man of the regional to consider investing five dollars per month for this work.

In accepting the appointment as assistant director, Donald Strunk "presented the challenge and vision of NICE, and the need to venture forward by faith to accept the opportunities being presented in both metropolitan and rural areas."

Missionary reports were given by Wesley and Norma Mansfield concerning growth at Carlton; by Gordon and Lorraine Titus of God's blessing at Lookingglass, Oregon; and by Roy and Elvia Sprague, mission evangelist, who had conducted meetings in nineteen different communities or churches.

At the next meeting of the board in April 1962, decisions were made relative to the training of Donald Strunk and the transfer of ministry leadership. Some of the concerns discussed were:

- Deputation and finances
- Help to missionaries and churches
- Accountability to the board and supporters
- Housing and office expense

- Travel expense
- Relationship between the director and the assistant director

The board urged the assistant director "to emphasize getting out into the churches to encourage the establishment of new churches, and to reach neglected areas especially."

During the year, God blessed the work of the mission and the missionaries in new areas such as Ashford, Boston Harbor, Allen, Bear Creek, and Fairview.

At the October 1962 IFCA regional conference at the Calvary Bible Church of Wenatchee, Washington, Reverend Donald R. Strunk was appointed to serve as the director of the Northwest Independent Church Extension. That action of the regional was acknowledged with deep gratitude to the Lord for the ministry of Henry and Margaret Boyd and with commitment of prayer and support for Don and Joanne Strunk. Rev. Wallace Wilson, board vice president, led in the prayer of installation for the Strunks. Don announced that his theme verse for this ministry would be "Serve the Lord with gladness" (Ps. 100:2).

Reverend and Mrs. Donald Strunk,
and Kathy

Chapter 5

Serving with Gladness

The hand of God upon the ministry of Don and Joanne Strunk as mission director was quickly evident. During the year, they traveled to churches throughout the Pacific Northwest, bringing a message concerning "the cycle of a New Testament church." Don used a chart which portrayed this cycle based on 1 Corinthians 3:5–9:

Who then is Paul, and who is Apollos, but ministers through whom you believed? I have planted, Apollos watered, but God gave the increase. So then neither he who plants is anything, nor he who waters, but God who gives the increase. Now he who plants and he who waters are one, and each one will receive his own reward according to his own labor. For we are God's fellow workers; you are God's field, you are God's building.

When reflecting on this time recently, Joanne said, "I marvel that as many times as I heard that message, that no two were ever alike. Don always adapted his illustrations to the area where we were, whether it was in wheat country and increase being bushels per acre, or apple orchards and props under the limbs."

Don had the desire to see churches planted in every community. He would scout out a community and then begin to pray for God's direction to meet the need. Joanne remembers that "we never went on a trip anywhere, vacation or otherwise, without checking on what churches were in the area sometime on the trip"

During 1963 and 1964, Don traveled to many Bible schools to present the work of the mission. His enthusiasm and vision were used of the Lord to challenge several couples to apply for service. Thus, new fields of ministry were opened, and new churches began.

Don's report to the regional that fall indicated he had represented the mission in forty-six meetings and had written eleven hundred letters. His work with pastoral search committees in eighteen churches resulted in their calling the men suggested. A mission policy book was prepared and used for the first time in 1964.

New Leaders, New Ministries

This was also a time for changes in the mission's leadership as new board members were elected by the IFCA regional. They were:

- Rev. Glenn Davis–Melrose Community Church
- Rev. Calvin Harrah–Calvary Bible Church
- Rev. Arnold Wall–Navy Yard City Bible Church
- Rev. Virgil Vater–Boulevard Baptist Church

Early in 1965 several new ministry opportunities gave much cause for rejoicing. One of these, "the Sequim Bible Church, grew out of the clear teaching of the Word by Rev. Andrew Olsen, a retired, fundamental Methodist preacher—Noel Olsen's father. The Legion Hall was rented and on February 4, 1965 the church was born. A total of thirty adults signed the charter membership registry."

There was much praise to God as their testimonies were shared with the board of NICE. From this humble beginning, God has built a growing church of over 500 believers that has impacted much of the Sequim Valley with the gospel and now supports more than twenty missionaries throughout the world.

Some of the other new opportunities in 1965 were at Mazama, Keller, and Mansfield, Washington, and at Canby, California. As a result of Don Strunk's aggressive efforts in recruiting, there were fourteen summer missionaries who were used of God to lead eighty-five precious souls to faith in Christ.

Concerning one of these summer missionaries, Don wrote, "Our trial of faith award goes to Doug Nichols, as his ministry at North River was invaluable in spite of many reverses that ended with a car accident at the Bible camp."

Little did anyone realize then that God would lead Doug Nichols to the Philippines, where he and his wife Margaret would be used of God to begin a ministry to street people. This work has grown into the worldwide outreach known as Action International Ministries. Recently, Doug Nichols commented, "My summer of training with NICE was invaluable preparation for the work God had planned for me; His way is perfect."

The Cornerstone Corps

The need to have a source of funds for church building projects resulted in the beginning of the NICE Cornerstone Corps in 1966. There were soon over fifty individuals who made a commitment to contribute to each call for building funds. The North River Community Church was the first project to receive Cornerstone Corps funds.

In the years since then, calls have been issued for nineteen different church building projects, and over $90,000 has been disbursed to help purchase property, or to build church facilities.

NICE Pastors

In May of 1966, the board of directors approved the status of NICE pastor, as one who is serving a church that has grown beyond the need of missionary support but still desires the help and ministry of the mission until the work is fully established.

Director Don Strunk reported to the regional in October 1966 that "the Lord has given a very fruitful and busy year, with six new missionaries and fourteen summer workers. I'm glad to be serving the Lord with NICE!" The board also approved the beginning of Operation Philip, to encourage IFCA pastors, and to help and strengthen churches where the mission is serving. A packet of informational items concerning the mission was distributed by the director—twenty-five pages of valuable and useful material!

Though the ministry of NICE was prospering under the Strunk's leadership, it still did not have the financial support necessary for them to devote full-time to the work. The president, Noel Olsen, sent a letter to all the churches, stating, "We thank God for our director and his wife and for their sacrificial ministry during these past five years. Reverend Strunk has been working faithfully for less than one dollar per hour in this tremendous missionary ministry. I am sure that you and your church will want to consider a wise investment for eternity through NICE."

Several individuals and churches responded to this appeal. And God continued to prosper the work with souls saved and growth in the churches.

Ten Years Of Blessing

As the tenth year of ministry came to a close in 1967, a new brochure that listed new goals for the year ahead was proposed and distributed. Those included a challenge:

- Believe God for more missionaries and church planters
- Ask God to open new doors for gospel outreach

At the IFCA regional meeting the entire time assigned to NICE was spent in praise for His hand of blessing, and prayer for even greater impact of the gospel throughout the Pacific Northwest.

As the ministry continued to grow, a wide variety of matters required the attention of the board. Things such as:

- Missionaries needing a license to preach
- Churches needing to be built
- Dealing with problem situations
- Vehicles needing repairs
- How to fund deputation trips
- How to accept title to a closed church
- Printing of missionary prayer cards
- Free—a used mimeograph machine
- Orientation for new workers
- Printing of the NICE Sender

- Canadian tax registration
- Need of missionary reports

The year 1968 began with a request from Don Strunk, to function in a dual role as Pastor of the Evergreen Bible Church of Vancouver, Washington, as well as director of the mission. Equal time would be given to each.

At the March board meeting the director reported that my "deputation trip to Bible schools and seminaries resulted in thirty-nine serious prospects for NICE ministry. But the bus ride was long, and I'm having some health problems."

Much time was spent by the leadership of the mission in preparation for the IFCA national convention, which would be hosted by Highlands Community Church in Renton during June 1968. The hours of planning were apparent, and the presence of God evident during this first ever Pacific Northwest IFCA national convention. The ministry of NICE was featured during the convention and was well received. To God be the glory, great things He has done!

New Challenges

As 1969 began, the director reported to the board that applications had been received from five couples for missionary service. One of these expressed interest in planting a church in the black community of Seattle. The board also approved scheduling worker conferences for NICE missionaries in several selected locations.

The work of the mission was growing and reaching into new areas. However, as Board President Wallace Wilson stated, "the mission is in transition, the Evergreen

Bible Church is in transition, and a man is in transition, namely Don." He continued, "A mission, a man, and a church all growing and maturing at the same time, presents a challenge to us to relieve Don from being worked to death." Following much discussion, the board approved another year of dual ministry for Don Strunk as NICE director and Evergreen Bible Church pastor.

The statement made in Acts 16:5—"churches established, increasing in number"—continued to be the experience of the missionaries with NICE.

In January 1970, the board received a letter from Don Strunk indicating his "confidence that a transfer of mission leadership is within the revealed will of God." In his letter he gave several suggestions relative to searching for God's man as the new director. With these, Don offered help and assistance during the time of transition. His letter concluded with an expression of praise, stating, "Truly, the past eleven years have been profitable to my wife and to me in our ministry, as we have been fellow laborers with NICE, serving the Lord with gladness!"

Their Ministry Continues

Don and Joanne continued their relationship with the mission for a total of twenty-five years, serving pastorates in Washington, Idaho, and Oregon. Don completed his doctoral thesis on the subject "911 for the Small Church," and received a doctor of ministry degree in February 1996.

Don was pastor of the First Baptist Church of South Bend, Washington for eleven years. He was called home to glory in September 1996 while on a hunting trip in Alaska. Joanne stated recently, "Don had a great heart to see people saved. Just a few weeks before the trip to Alaska, he had such a burden for the lost of the community that he mentioned in his message one Sunday that if it took his death to reach this community for Christ, it would be worth it. God is using Don's death for His honor and glory."

Don and Joanne's son, Terry, with his wife Lisa and family, are NICE missionaries serving the North River Bible Church. Joanne is again serving with the mission as a special missionary.

Jerry and Lois James, Lemuel, Nathan, and Jenny, 1979

Dr. and Mrs. Donald Strunk, 1996

Gordon and Lorraine Titus

Don Strunk, Henry Boyd, and Roy Sprague
The Three Directors

Chapter 6

More Than Just a Job

With the resignation of Don Strunk, the board of directors prayerfully sought God's guidance to the man of His choice to provide leadership for the mission. At a specially called meeting, the board took action to "contact Roy Sprague, relative to the possibility of him serving as director for NICE."

That contact was made and Elvia and I began to pray, "Lord, if this is Your will, please make it so clear that there is no way that we'll miss it."

I spent time in fasting, prayer, and reading the Word. And never before, or since, has the witness of the Holy Spirit been so clear to me. There were two verses which seemed to jump off the page as I read and prayed. The first was John 10:4; "And when He putteth forth His own sheep, He goeth before them; and the sheep follow Him . . . " And the second, "As you go, your way shall be opened up step by step before you" (Prov. 4:12 NASV).

Thus ,when Wallace Wilson, Bernard LeRoy, and Noel Olsen met with me to ask "are you interested?" my answer was already certain. "Yes, there is no question! God is leading us." They stated that they did not know what the financial support would be, since the previous month's receipts in the general fund had been just $245, but if God was leading, He would supply.

I can remember replying, "If the mission will pay the expenses of the ministry we will trust God for our needs, even if the salary is zero. I view this as more than just a job, it's a call from God."

At the IFCA regional conference in March 1970, at Memorial Bible Church in Yakima, "a motion was made by Ernest Quaintance and seconded by Gordon Titus that a call be extended to Roy Sprague to serve as the Director of NICE." It was approved unanimously.

Rev. Richard Schwab and Rev. Noel Olsen spoke concerning the need to pray for and support the ministry of the new director. Several of the brethren made a promise of their financial investment, and many indicated their commitment to pray. The meeting concluded with prayer led by one of the mission's founders, Rev. Charles Lyman. The mission had an excellent foundation and a good reputation.

Many Things New

There was the need of a new office—in the Sprague's home; a new address—a post office box in Mountlake Terrace, Washington; a new phone number—the Sprague's; new literature printed with these changes; and a new financial secretary—God provided Rev. Harold Davey, a man with a heart for missions and a man of prayer. The supplying hand of the Lord was very evident!

The board of directors urged the Spragues to make their top priority twofold:

1. Visit all the NICE missionaries as often as possible
2. Seek to schedule meetings in as many churches as possible for the purpose of promotion and support

Almost before things were ready in the new mission office, contacts were received asking for help in starting two new churches—one in Twin falls, Idaho and the other in Council, Idaho. While meeting with the believers at Council, a phone call was placed to Don and Carol Martin asking them to consider this pioneer ministry. With their baby due to be born on Tuesday, it was astounding to the folks that Don would come over on Monday to meet with them. This willingness did something for their faith that is hard to express. And Council Bible Church was planted!

At the fall IFCA regional conference, a report was presented to the members, giving thanks to God for the faithfulness of the mission's twenty-one families as they served in areas of spiritual need. The announcement of the beginning of the NICE Youth Corps was made, and pastors and churches were urged to pray and to become involved.

At this same time, October 1970, a monthly mission family letter was begun, which has continued to the present. In the first issue of *The NICE Digest*, I wrote, "Both Elvia and I sincerely thank you and thank the Lord for your warm acceptance of our ministry with you as director. We always want to be available to help in every way that we can—our full time will be devoted to the ministry of NICE. Let me know whenever I can assist you with evangelism, training, conferences, or in any way. We're glad to be laborers together."

An article in the first *NICE Digest* quoted Psalm 73; "My flesh and my heart faileth; *but God* is the strength of my heart and my portion forever."

The article continued with these words of encouragement, "Yes, the godless do prosper. We may suffer loss because of godliness and integrity. *But God* is our guide now and has prepared glory for us hereafter. Our heart would faint—*but God* is our strength! Our flesh would fail—*but God* is our portion forever!"

Roy and Elvia Sprague
and Monica and Judith in 1961.

Attitude Check

Two very significant avenues of God's blessing were launched in 1971. These two—NICE Youth Corps and NICE Partners In Faith—touched many lives and were used to strengthen the ministry of the mission.

In January the first Partners in Faith banquets were held. Those featured a film presentation concerning the mission, testimonies of God's working, and a message titled "Tending to Business", by Dr. Lowell Wendt. There were almost 200 people in attendance at each one in Portland and Seattle.

The director conducted a series of evangelistic meetings at Chapel of the Cascades in Bend, where God brought touches of revival, with *eighteen* decisions for Christ. Fred Curow reported from Cambridge, Idaho that "we've got to build; we have Sunday school classes being held all over town." Earl and Shirley Brubaker were praising God for the response to the Extra Effort program on Mondays at Columbia View. Jerry and Lois James found the happy hour Bible clubs to be a means of growth at Rosewood Chapel. And David Kerns conducted a baptismal service for ten new believers at Hope, Idaho. The faithfulness of those serving with the mission has been a continuing factor through the years.

During May, four of the board members made a tour to seven fields of ministry. In fact, Noel Olsen, Bill Cross, Roland Frederick, and Roy Sprague formed The NICE Quartet and sang on several occasions during this trip.

The first year of the NICE Youth Corps there were twenty teens who enrolled in study and preparation for mission outreach, during the summer. They learned how to do visitation evangelism, how to share their faith, how to conduct a youth rally, and how to lead a person to Christ.

During the day, in fact, many times each day, one of the teens of the youth corps team would shout, "attitude check," and then the entire group would answer in unison, "praise the Lord!"

As the teens would come to a church where NICE missionaries were serving, they would work with the local young people in a program of skits, games, testimonies, and evangelism called a youth-a-rama. They would plan the program during the day, pray a lot, and go from door to door in the afternoon to invite other teens to the rally that night. There were six youth-a-ramas conducted during 1971 with over seventy decisions made for Christ. The leadership for the teams was provided by Joann Coffield and Philip Kirsch.

Don Martin reported from Council, Idaho, that four college girls gave a public testimony of their faith following a youth-a-rama. He added, "We have had several outstanding services in our short history as a church, but this was the greatest yet!"

From 1971 to 1976, the Lord blessed and used the NICE Youth Corps in a most significant way. There were almost

400 teens who professed Christ as savior! Even more thrilling is the fact that fifty-four of the sixty-two teens who were a part of the youth corps during those years enrolled in Bible colleges to prepare for Christian service.

Attitude is not only important for young people but is of tremendous significance for all of God's servants. It's been said, attitude is everything!

God Answers Prayer

In 1971 for the first time, the NICE Board met for two days of prayer. This is a time when the board of directors, together with their wives, meet to focus on praise and to petition for the entire mission family. What a tremendous source of refreshing this has been each year since.

This prompted the beginning of the NICE prayer partners—people who have made a commitment to pray daily for the work of God through the mission. Over and again, people have stated, "I pray for NICE every day." These people are sent the "Praise and Prayer Report" each month, which lists answers to prayer and specific needs for the churches and for the missionaries. Indeed, "The effectual, fervent prayer of a righteous man availeth much" (James 5:16).

Many times I've been asked, what is the mission's greatest need. And always the answer is prayer—more prayer! As our brother Bill Cross has said many times, "Pray for me more than you do!"

Truly, the harvest is great. God says the answer, the source of power, the source of provision is, "Pray the Lord of the harvest" (Matt. 9:38).

Bill and Joy Cross

Chapter 8

Vignettes of Praise

Call unto Me, and I will answer thee, and show thee
great and mighty things. . . . (Jer. 33:3)

God does not anoint methods. He anoints men and
women to do a job for Him.

The mid 1970s were years of many opportunities and constant provision from the Lord. No evidence of His provision was any greater than His call to many men and women to serve with the mission.

In 1958 a total of five missionaries served with NICE. That number had grown to twenty-one in 1968, and to one hundred and five by 1978.

1972

During the year, there were Partners in Faith banquets held in Seattle, Portland, Port Angeles, Spokane, Grants Pass, Burney, Wenatchee, and Yakima. In each one, testimonies were given of God's blessing in people's lives, of new churches started, and of souls saved. The attendance was very good at each location, and the love offering received covered the expenses. The banquets had truly become an enjoyable time of fellowship, and an occasion to share the challenge of church extension.

God's provision was evidenced by:

- 5 new churches started
- 13 new missionaries accepted to serve
- Safety in travel to 6 Bible colleges
- Office rented for the mission
- Brubakers appointed as field director
- 7 young people enrolling in Bible colleges
- 113 teens trusting Christ in youth-a-ramas

The home Bible classes for nonbelievers at Chelan, Washington were used to bring several people to Christ. "A man gave his orchard to God last Sunday," wrote Homer Poland concerning their ministry at Rock Island, Washington.

For the first time, NICE was able to hire a secretary— Joann Coffield. The faithfulness and expertise of each of the secretaries who have served in the office since has contributed greatly to the effectiveness of the mission's work. Through the years, Virginia Kennedy, Elvia Sprague, Judy Doyle, MaryAnn Marion, Liz Coffman, Claudia Walling, Judi Allen, and Shirley Brubaker have capably fulfilled this responsibility.

1973

Again there were Partners in Faith banquets held, some of them in new locations. At Council, there were seventy-seven people in attendance, and one man stood to his feet and said, "God has greatly blessed our Church, and the entire town has had a spiritual awakening!"

There were three cars donated for use by missionaries in need. The fiscal year ended with all funds showing a positive balance for the first time in fourteen years!

To celebrate the fifteenth anniversary the theme "Let Us Go On . . . " was chosen as a challenge to believe God for greater usefulness. And Project 7 was adopted as a focus and goal for seven new ministries each year of the 1970s.

Myrl and Judy Root accepted a call to serve the Happy Camp Bible Church. A youth corps team was scheduled to help them in making an initial contact with the community. Myrl wrote, "At the beginning of the week we were led to claim fifteen teens for Christ; our people had a big question, 'How could this happen in Happy Camp?' Well, by Thursday night the youth corps team had led fifteen precious teens to Christ! Praise God, He answers!"

In fact, there were a total of 134 teenagers who professed Christ through the youth corps that year. There were four new couples accepted to serve with the mission.

1974

"God grant us the grace and strength to view this year as one of great opportunity for the glory of the Lord," were the words I wrote to the mission family as the year began.

Truly His provision was abundant:

- Strunks appointed as Idaho field director
- New parsonage completed at Coal Creek
- 7 new ministries begun
- 18 youth-a-ramas conducted with 103 teens professing Christ as savior
- 13 new missionaries accepted for service

One of the new missionary couples, Vince and Brenda Ortiz, desired to move to a city where there was both need and potential. Our surveys indicated Oak Harbor, Washington was the place. With fear, and much faith, they rented a home, began to contact people, and pray! Their first convert was a seven year old neighbor girl who asked, "Please tell me about Jesus."

With considerable boldness, they visited the mayor, chief of police, and superintendent of schools. Many people in the community became aware of their presence. A local school was rented, and the Family Bible Church began— with six people the first Sunday and thirteen the second.

Bob and Anita Ohlson came to serve the church in 1981, and God has mightily used them to impact this military town with the gospel. The church has ventured to reach the military personnel, sought to train them, and then allow the government to send them around the world as missionaries!

There have been many challenges to faith through the years, but today the church has three worship services and ministers to almost 700 people.

No Gas!

God's provision is amazing even in the small things. My daughter Judi and I took the mission's Mobile Chapel to Idaho and then had a NICE Sunday at the Onecho Bible Church near Colfax, Washington. We had to be home Monday morning, so we started out after the evening service trusting that there would be a gas station open along the way. (These were the days of gas shortage) But, even the truck stations had signs "NO GAS."

I knew I couldn't make it home without more gas—what should we do? We prayed and drove on, and the tank kept getting closer to empty. As I neared the rest area near Cle Elum, I felt impressed to pull in, and at almost midnight there was one car there. As I got out of the truck, I noticed that the man with the car had a gas can.

Somewhat embarrassed, I asked if he could sell us some gas. He answered, "Oh, I suppose so." And then I noticed he had three five-gallon gas cans. He asked what we were doing, and I told him we had taken a Mobile Chapel to Idaho. I learned that he lived in Oak Harbor. He was quite interested that NICE was starting a church there. He not only put five gallons in the tank but refused to let me pay, saying, "Just put it in the offering." We drove on, overwhelmed at God's wonderful provision.

1975

When the title of this book was chosen, I had totally forgotten that in 1975 I suggested the following goals for the year:

1. Ask God for vision to see His purpose
2. Believe God to venture forth trusting Him
3. Praise God as He brings the victories

Truly, God's faithfulness was evident:

- 6 new churches started
- James and Shinns appointed field directors
- Wall appointed missionary at large
- 18 new missionaries accepted
- Mobile home given to start a church
- 37 baptisms reported

1976

"May Christ be all-sufficient, as you serve Him with renewed vision and commitment in 1976," was the prayer expressed, as I wrote to the mission family to begin the year.

The Wards rejoiced in three adults saved and four baptized at Carson Bible Church. The Shinns started summer Bible camps with 147 attending, and the church in Reno adopted its charter membership. The Nashes were blessed by $8,000 being given for down payment on property in Ellensburg. The Chisms praised God for two ladies Bible studies starting. The Grahams wrote, "God has blessed us by directing the city council to allow a variance for use of our warehouse church; we have three new families, and ten people were recently baptized."

There were twenty-one new missionaries accepted during the year, and thirty-nine churches were now being served. Truly, it was God's work!

Chapter 9

Come Over and Help Us

There stood a man of Macedonia, and prayed him,
saying, Come over . . . and help us. (Acts 16:9)

The response of the mission to begin ministry in the
Sierra Nevada area was a great step of faith. There
had been requests for help four years earlier, but without
the needed leadership it seemed impossible. Then when
God directed Garland and Roberta Shinn to plant the Faith
Bible Church in Reno, the board requested that he also
serve as field director. It was apparent that this was God's
provision.

Early in 1977, a request came from the IFCA regional
in Arizona, asking "Can you help us organize and begin a
church extension ministry here?" Obviously, the distance
from the Pacific Northwest made such involvement imprac-
tical. Yet, the burden to plant and establish churches wherever needed influenced the director to spend a week in
Arizona to encourage, counsel, help, and pray with the
brethren concerning the development of a church extension mission. This time of sharing was instrumental, in part,
to the organization of the Southwest Bible Church Mission.

NICE continued to minister aggressively in the Pacific Northwest. The goals for the year were for ten new ministries and twelve new missionaries.

The reports indicated there were:

- High school coaches saved at Winnemucca
- Men taking leadership at Coal Creek
- New people attending at Reno
- People praying regularly at Rock Island
- 8 new churches begun
- 20 new missionaries appointed to service

With a burden for a needy state, John and Jane Edgell requested the blessing of NICE to move to West Virginia to start a church extension mission.

The director met with the IFCA regional in Montana to discuss the development of church extension there. By unanimous vote of the regional, NICE was asked to direct the ministry of church extension in Montana, and Gene and Norma Greyn were appointed as field director.

After Twenty Years

As the mission began its twentieth year, the evidence was overwhelming that God was indeed building His church. Since its inception, there had been seventy-seven churches planted or established by the 105 missionaries, and another 212 churches served in a variety of ministries of assistance and growth. "Great is the Lord, and greatly to be praised" (Ps. 145:3).

During the year, twenty-eight Partners in Faith praise banquets were held throughout the Northwest. An informative and challenging film titled *God Uses Ordinary*

People was presented. In a graphic way, this gave testimony of the work God had done through the mission, and the people who had a part: missionaries, music leaders, janitors, Sunday school teachers, prayer warriors, youth leaders, construction workers, bus drivers, board members, pianists, nursery workers—*all,* God's servants.

Because of these willing people, and their faithfulness to their Lord, there were ten new ministries and eight new missionaries in 1978.

A Decade of Growth

The church extension committee of the Gulf States regional of IFCA requested the loan of a church planter/mission director to develop a mission in their area. By faith, Jerry and Lois James answered this call, and in August 1979 moved to Birmingham, Alabama. By the end of the year, one church was started and surveys were conducted in three other communities.

At this time, NICE was renting two small rooms in Mountlake Terrace for the mission office. Thus, the board of directors at their annual meeting adopted Project '79 as a commitment to trust God to provide a permanent headquarters. They began to investigate potential sites, and urged people in all the churches to pray for God's provision.

As the decade drew to a close, the mission and its leaders were in awe at the abundance of God's blessing. We asked God for seventy new ministries in the 1970s, which seemed an incredible request, but the records of the ten years indicated that there were new ministries in 31 communities in Washington, 16 in Oregon, 11 in Idaho, 7 in Nevada, 4 in Montana, and 2 in California—a total of 71 in the 1970s!

Of these, thirty-one were new church plants, and forty were struggling churches in which a missionary had been placed. God alone knows the number of souls saved and lives transformed by the power of the gospel. "Lord, Thou art worthy, to receive glory and honor . . . " (Rev. 4:11).

Chapter 10

Not a Penny of Debt

Owe no man anything; but to love one another.
(Romans 13:8).

The goals adopted by the board of directors for the new decade were staggering—except for the fact of a great God! They were:

- 80 new ministries in the 1980s
- 80 new missionaries in the 1980s
- 800 Partners in Faith in the 1980s (those who will pray for NICE daily)
- 8 additional field directors
- Provision of a mission evangelist and an assistant director
- Provision of a headquarters building

In regard to these goals, it was acknowledged by the board "that we recognize our total insufficiency in ourselves to accomplish these things; they can only be reached as we are totally dependent upon Christ to work through us."

Valuable Ministries

The service to established churches of providing pastoral placement information and help has been extremely valuable through the years. Since 1970, each year an average of thirty churches and forty men have been served in this manner. The mission personnel provides counsel to churches needing a pastor and supplies informational resumes of qualified godly men who are available as candidates. That service has been provided to almost 300 churches since 1958.

The mission's printing ministry is another avenue of service to the churches and missionaries. God graciously supplied the needed funds to purchase an offset printing press and darkroom equipment to facilitate that work. Mr. Art Mc Connaughey served as mission printer for several years. During that time, he taught the director how to be a printer—most of the time I'm thankful for this!

The board approved the following policy concerning printing to be done by the mission:

1. Prayer cards and prayer letters for missionaries will be prepared, printed, and mailed without cost;
2. Printing of leaflets, brochures, letterheads, and other items for mission churches will be provided at the cost of materials

A Headquarters Building

During 1980, God's provision was thrilling! Bill Cross was appointed as administrative assistant, and in answer to prayer, the Sunset Bible Church of University Place (Tacoma) gave to NICE a parcel of land on which the board of directors authorized the construction of a mission headquarters building.

On November 1, 1980, a ground breaking service was held, and many people, including children, participated in turning shovels of earth.

A series of Partners in Faith banquets were held in almost thirty locations during the fall of 1980. The provision of property for the mission headquarters was shared, and the challenge to construct the building with volunteer labor was presented. As a result, many people from many churches responded—an architect, a contractor, painters, roofers, decorators, all willing servants! And the film story *Love This World through Me* kept the purpose of NICE in primary focus. God blessed with nine new ministries during the year.

In December, the plans for the thirty-two foot by seventy-two foot building with a full basement were submitted to the Pierce County planning department. A report sent to the churches in January 1981 stated "there have been several special answers to prayer, involving the fire department and department of public works; and now, after several weeks of delay, approval has been granted, and the long-awaited construction will begin!"

And God's people were ready! Some gave materials, some provided their expertise, some invested money, and some donated their time. As a result, the 4,300 square foot headquarters building was constructed without a penny of indebtedness. That building, now valued at $400,000, was built at a total cost of $71,000, because God's people had a mind to work. Some worked a few hours, and others like Jack Clapp, Maco Allason, Wayne Stewart, and Bill Cross spent months working day after day.

One Thursday, the trusses were to be delivered at 9:00 A.M. What were we to do with them? We had no one with that kind of expertise. A crew of men from Country

Bible Church of Enumclaw arrived at 8:30 A.M., asking,
"Is there anything we can do today to help?" Unknown
to anyone, except the Lord, these men regularly installed
building trusses. By the end of the day all the trusses
were in place and were ready for roofing. One of the men
commented, "Wow, God is building this place!"

The building was ready for use by February 1982.
Several trips with borrowed trucks moved all the
mission's belongings to Tacoma and into the new building. The Spragues moved to a nearby apartment.

On May 1, 1982 the headquarters building was completed and a service of dedication conducted. Truly,
"this is the Lord's doing; it is marvelous in our eyes"
(Ps. 118:23).

Garland and Roberta Shinn

Mission Headquarters Building

Bob and Anita Ohlson and Laura, 1977

Frank and Wendy Emrich

Chapter 11

Exceeding, Abundantly

> Now unto Him who is able to do exceeding, abun-
> dantly, above all that we ask or think. (Eph. 3:20)

In answer to prayer, Willard English came to serve as the financial secretary. Through the years, God has provided His man for this vital work—each at just the right time— Jim Coffman, then Earl Brubaker, and Bob Allen.

Indeed, 1982 was a year of much blessing. An eighty-six year old man in Idaho trusted Christ. A young man in Oregon said, "I won't need this statue in my truck anymore, because now I have Jesus Christ in my life." There were three new churches planted in Nevada. The construction of five new church buildings began. The Coal Creek Church developed a radio ministry. God directed twelve new missionaries to serve with NICE.

After Twenty-five Years

The twenty-fifth year brought many occasions of rejoicing. There were Partners in Faith banquets or rallies conducted in forty-two locations in the six states where the mission serves. At those, testimonies were given of people who came to know Christ, of many who had been taught the Word of God, and of some who were preparing to enter into Christian service. A new multimedia presentation titled *Glorify Thy Name in All the Earth* was also featured. The special speakers for those celebrations of praise were Dr. John F. Walvoord, Dr. Alden Gannett, Dr. Harold Longenecker, Dr. Lowell Wendt, Rev. Noel Olsen, and Rev. Ron Eggert.

During that anniversary year, there were three issues of *The Increase*. The emphasis was on praise to God! And each issue also gave a challenge:

1. To reach into the next towns
2. To develop balanced churches
3. To reach out and touch someone for Christ

God led twenty-four new missionaries into service during the year, and there were nine new ministries!

A unique cookbook was compiled in 1983, with recipes from all the missionary ladies—almost 1000 copies were sold! The proceeds from that project were used to purchase cupboards and appliances for the headquarters kitchen.

The anniversary year concluded with a Gene Emry steak barbecue dinner for those of the NICE family who could attend. Poeschels reported seven professions of faith and six people baptized at Happy Camp. Casads told of fifteen people at Nehalem Valley trusting Christ. What a special occasion of reflection concerning God's faithfulness and the abundance of His blessing!

Chapter 12

Spirit Refreshers

... they have addicted themselves to ministry ... and they
have refreshed my spirit and yours (1 Cor. 16:17–18).

Four teenagers and one elderly man have been saved,
and one of our families is growing strong in the Lord,"
reported the Benthiens as 1984 began. The Wentworths
wrote, "We praise God for the spiritual growth we are seeing in so many young believers." The Cornells shared, "several new families are attending, and we're starting men's
Bible studies."

In 1985, five new churches began and six new missionaries started their service with NICE. The Marvins
wrote, "One of our Onion Creek couples is going to Bible
school!" The total of all reports from the churches indicated that 211 children professed Christ as savior during
the summer Bible clubs and vacation Bible schools.
"Glory!" was the response of Noel Olsen, when he heard
these reports at the meeting of the board.

During 1986, the records indicate that there were
seven new ministries and eighteen new missionaries approved for service.

Workers Together

There is no limit to what can be done,
if it doesn't matter who gets the credit.

That statement has been demonstrated again and again by the workers and churches that are a part of NICE. The beginning of branch churches; the investing of workers to help a new church; the gift of pews and hymnals; the donation of a vehicle; the hours spent in building construction—those are just some of the ways the people of the Northwest have met needs and provided encouragement.

In fact, through the years there has been an increasing number of faithful financial supporters of Northwest Independent Church Extension. Those people, through their regular monetary contributions, enable the mission and the missionaries to accomplish the work of church extension. To those co-laborers in the gospel, my deepest gratitude!

The board of directors and the mission family absolutely stunned the director at the fall IFCA regional conference in 1986. Board President Ron Eggert took over the meeting and indicated that the NICE family were giving Elvia and me a trip to Israel! And then we became speechless when a video was played of President Cook of BIOLA University informing me that I was to be granted an honorary doctor of divinity degree at the spring commencement!

A close friend asked how I felt about receiving that honor. I answered, "I believe this is not only for me, but also an expression to all the men and women of NICE who labor so faithfully— often times unnoticed by the world at large." We are, indeed, richly blessed!

Servant Leaders

From its inception, the mission leaders have been devoted to serving the missionaries and churches. It's been said that a servant is one who seeks to make others successful. One of the greatest joys in the ministry is to see men and women become fruitful in the work of the Lord.

The board of directors desires to do everything possible to encourage, counsel, assist, train, help, and equip missionaries for effective service. Their appointment of godly leaders has resulted in expansion and effectiveness of the mission's ministry. Through the years, there have been:

- 25 field directors
- 4 missionaries at large
- Noel and Lorraine Olsen, mission pastor
- Lowell and Marie Wendt, representative
- Bob and Judi Allen, ethnic director
- Earl and Shirley Brubaker, John and Jane Edgell, assistant directors

These servants of the Lord have been my greatest encouragement in the ministry. They have formed a team of leadership and are indeed addicted to ministry. They are spirit refreshers!

Gene and Norma Greyn

Ernest and Donna Quaintance, 1994

Part III

To Victory!

Charles and Alice Holgate, 1996

John and Jane Edgell

Chapter 13

Footprints to Follow

And ye became followers of us, and of the Lord . . . .
(1 Thess.1:6).

The Word of God declares our task: disciple the nations. Scripture defines our strategy: penetrate the world with the gospel. And our Lord has demonstrated the results: the formation of His Body, the church.

During the decade of the 80s, God used the mission and its missionaries to plant thirty-eight new churches and to place missionary pastors in twenty-eight struggling churches. God is building His church!

Opportunities in View

The Apostle Paul wrote, "For a great door and effectual is opened unto me; and there are many adversaries" (1 Cor. 16:9). He was declaring a basic philosophy of ministry. The difference between defeat and victory often depends on whether our focus is on the difficulties, or the opportunities. The emphasis of NICE has always been on the open doors, rather than the obstacles. At times, there have been difficulties and disappointments. But time and again, God has proven His sufficiency!

Missions at Our Doorstep

King Solomon petitioned the Lord at the dedication of the temple, praying " . . . that all people of the earth may know thy Name" (1 Kings 8:43). As the mission began 1990, the board of directors boldy declared that "NICE must use every means possible to reach the mission field at our doorstep, the unreached ethnic communities." Throughout the six states, people were urged to pray for workers who would reach the ethnic communities.

The first answer to these prayers was the Lord's direction in 1992 to Bob and Judi Allen to serve as director of ethnic ministries. In 1994, Jesús and Maria Cordova moved to the Yakima area as Hispanic field director. What God has done through them is exciting:

- 3 Spanish speaking churches
- Over 300 Hispanics trusted Christ
- 30+ believers baptized
- 2 men being trained for ministry

In 1998, the Valley Bible Church of Sumner, Washington began an Hispanic church through the leadership of retired missionaries Bob and Dawn Archer. God is at work!

We must continue to pray for church planters to reach into Asian communities, Afro-American communities, Hispanic communities, Native American communities, Russian communities—indeed, to *all* peoples!

Commitment to Biblical Principles

Beginning in 1988, the school of ministry has provided instruction for new missionaries. These servants of Christ are taught important biblical principles concerning such things as the church, ethics, integrity, pastoring, finances, marriage, and servant leadership.

One of the key ingredients of a growing church is a clearly defined purpose. When a church knows its purpose, it can identify its goals and set its priorities.

When church planters or missionary pastors move into a new community, they seek to build relationships that will develop ministry. They declare the true gospel—the *bad* news that people are lost and without hope, and the *good* news of salvation by grace through faith. As God draws people to Himself, the missionary seeks to ground them in the Word, thus making disciples of Jesus Christ.

The Wisdom Of Age

Sometimes older missionaries feel as though they have been "put out to pasture." What a tragedy to lose the valuable wisdom and example of these servants of the Lord. Their years of experience have given them insight and perspective on life and ministry that is priceless. NICE seeks to provide opportunities of service for those who are retired, and thus enriching many individuals and churches.

Don and Jody Wantland

Bob and Judi Allen, David and Rachel

Chapter 14

Great Is Thy Faithfulness

Thy faithfulness is unto all generations.
(Ps. 119:90).

God is faithful in providing men and women to serve Him. God is faithful in directing and sustaining His servants. God is faithful in bringing spiritual fruit from their ministries. We can trust Him for every situation in every generation.

The 1990s

The faithfulness of our God to NICE has been abundant to the present day. There have been seventy-two new missionaries and twenty-six new churches in the 1990s. There have been girls and boys, men and women saved. Believers have been baptized. Homes have been strengthened. Communities have been impacted by the gospel. Churches have been planted and developed. The glory is His alone!

On the following pages are reports from NICE missionaries and excerpts from their letters. God is at work! He is building His church!

Dear Family and Friends,

WOW we are so blessed!! This year has been a constant channel of blessing.

1. Our health has been good. Linda's headaches have decreased and are manageable.
2. Our house finally sold! Bless the Lord!
3. The ministry is going well. We have about ten new families represented in the congregation and six people have trusted Christ as their savior this year. Bless the Lord!
4. Finally, you, our loyal family and support team! Your faithfulness in praying, supporting, and encouraging us has been a blessing beyond measure. Bless the Lord!

—Larry & Linda Ott

Larry and Linda Ott

Jim and Kathy Miller,
Josh and Ruth Ann

Dear Praying Friends,
Saturday, February 21, 1998. Kathy calls me to the kitchen and there is a fellow I know only by reputation (and that reputation isn't good). We put a pot of coffee on and then sit at the table to talk. It seems he has had it with his life decisions and the direction he's going. Forty years of serving the Devil, he's at the end of his rope. He wants help. I'm sitting there thinking, *Oh boy, Oh boy, Oh boy, do I ever have the answer for you!* I was able to share with him the fact that what he needed was forgiveness. He had been running all his life away from God, now it was time to run to God! What a privilege to be able to show him the promises of Scripture concerning salvation. That afternoon in my kitchen Joe was born into God's family as he prayed to ask God to forgive him. I never cease to marvel at how God works. I challenged Joe to come to church and to share with the congregation what God had done. Sure enough, Sunday morning there's Joe with his wife, and He shared with the body of Christ how God had forgiven him. What an encouragement! As for us, we thank God for such an opportunity.
In Christ,
—Jim and Kathy Miller

Keith and Marnella Lyons

THE LYONS DEN
Dear Friends and Relatives,
God is blessing the ministry. August thrilled us with
VBS, and then September found us at the Harvest
Festival sharing the "Wordless Book" at the Child
Evangelism Fellowship tent. 258 children and adults
heard the story and 94 trusted Christ as their savior.
Our people involved are encouraged to see God work.
October brought us increase in our youth group and
our mailbox club. We are blessed because your gifts and
prayers make this possible. Pray for our Thanksgiving
service and dinner, and for our youth group which is
beginning to plan an all church Christmas program.
In Christ whom we serve,
—Keith & Marnella Lyons

Dear Praying Friends,

We are happy to report that we are alive and well here in Hobart, Washington. Remember when . . . we were excited about twenty people in Sunday morning worship? Average attendance is now between fifty-five and sixty. The Lord has added five babies, two families, and one couple to our congregation this year. Remember when . . . our youth programs needed structure? Eleven people are now working with Word of Life clubs begun just over two years ago. At least twelve teens and eight children have accepted Christ and many have followed the Lord in baptism. Remember when . . . we had more work than workers? We still do! But several families that have become members are a great help in many areas of ministry. This is the first year that all board positions have been filled.

We truly praise the Lord!

With love,

—Rob and Ruth Morris

Rob and Ruth Morris, Rick, Ryan, and Rachel

Dear Brethren in Christ,

In the month of March spring begins, and in the valley of Yakima it is still cold and it is expected to snow again. The flu at this time is very common.

But even through the flu and the cold, the people are still coming to church. In these past weeks, especially Wednesday night Bible study and Awana, the van has been completely full. Praise be to God! The state accepted our petition to incorporate the church and they have sent us a certificate of incorporation. The church is growing and we have need of biblical materials for the children.

PLEASE PRAY:

1. For two brethren that have decided to be baptized
2. For the vacation Bible school for the kids in Harrah
3. For another English speaking church to open their doors, so that we may start another Spanish church

Por amor a Cristo,
—Los Cordova

Jesùs and Maria Cordova

Dear Friends and Family Members,

God has been gracious to Christ The Savior Bible
Church. As a church plant, we have been able to reach
far more people than our size would normally dictate.
Two ministries within the church which excite me
are the One to One discipling and the ladies' Women
of Excellence study. Nancy leads the women's study,
and it's great to see their growth. One To One is being
done, mainly by the men of the church. Four men
have been through the discipling course, and now six
men/boys are being discipled. The growth and maturing in the Word is exciting.
Nancy and I want to thank you for your prayer
support and financial support. Without it, we would
not have been able to do what we have done. The
church has doubled in size from this time last year. As
God continues to bless us, we will not be a church
plant, but a planted church.

Love, from Chris and Nancy

Chris and Nancy McGreer

MULLINS MESSAGES

The other night at Bible study, someone asked me how I pick the subject matter for my messages. "If you see a problem with someone in the church, do you address that issue?" Behind that question was the power of the Word of God and the probing of the Spirit of God in the heart of that person.

I try to simply be faithful to preach and teach the Word of God in a personal and practical manner. The power of the Word is tremendous. It is able to judge the thoughts and intentions of the heart.

I am grateful for the occasions when He allows me to get a glimpse of what is happening in the heart of those we serve.

—Jeff, for the Mullins

STRUNK SPOTLIGHT

At the beginning of the year, Terry and I were questioning whether or not we had a ministry here. The Lord gave us a resounding Yes!

On January 15th we met a young lady who came to Terry with her final wishes, and a note to be read at her funeral. She planned to kill herself that night. By the time she left, she had given us her pills and alcohol and her promise that she would not hurt herself.

Since that time, we have spent countless hours counseling with her, and she has now committed her life to Christ. It's exciting to see her grow and desire to serve the Lord!

Please continue to pray for her as she grows in her faith and works through past issues.

—Lisa, for Terry and the troops

Dear Friends and Family,

I had stood in the hospital room when my son was born twenty-one years ago. Now I was standing in the funeral home at his casket. I placed my hands on his hands, and prayed, *"Lord, You gave him to us as a gift of Your love; I now give him back to You as an act of worship."*

With this prayer came release, and I experienced God's special comfort and sustaining grace. Jonathan's life had touched hundreds of young people with the love of Christ. Now in his death, hundreds more were confronted with the reality of life and death and eternity. In fact, since the funeral, there have been over seventy people come to Christ. And others who have come back to the Lord. It's amazing!

Our ministry, in this predominately German Catholic town, is through Koffee Konnection. The coffee shop is more and more a place to connect with people for the glory of God. We have new families coming to the services. God is at work. We understand now, so much more, what God did for us when He gave us His own Son. Thank you for your prayers and support—we need them at this time.

—Pastor Prentice, Louree and the Boyd family

Prentice and Louree Boyd, Tiffany,
Jonathan, Andrew, Daniel

THANK YOU

A missionary's human
To that I can attest.
He faces much discouragement
And difficulty—like the rest.
Serving in 'lonely places'
Yet not alone, we see,
For many faithful servants
Join the fight on bended knee.
How grateful we may be to God
For you, that prayerful one.
Who approached the Throne of Glory
In the Name of God's dear Son.
For your prayers and gracious giving,
For your laboring of love—
Rich rewards are surely waiting
For each one of you above.
But until that day triumphant
With a glad and grateful heart
We at NICE would like to tell you,
'THANK YOU for your part!'

—Celeste DeFord, NICE missionary
Ekalaka, Montana

Roy and Elvia Sprague

Lowell and Marie Wendt

Sequim Bible Church, Founded 1964

Family Bible Church of Oak Harbor, Founded 1974

Chapter 15

Time Is Running Out

Is time running out for America? Are these the last days? Just what time is it spiritually? Certainly the evidence is overwhelming that we may not have much longer to reach out with the gospel. The signs of the times point to the soon return of our Lord.

As we approach the year 2000, leading missiologists cite statistics that indicate an overwhelming response to the gospel throughout the world. People are turning to Christ in thrilling numbers in almost every country of the world—but not the United States of America.

It's true! Statistics reveal that approximatley 170 million people in the United States do not know our Savior. Even with all the churches that exist in America, and with all the Christian radio and TV programs, our beloved country is now the third largest spiritually unreached mission field in the world! Only India and China have more nonbelievers. Yes, the opportunity exists in the USA, but the response is apathetic.

In 1900, over 66 percent of Americans were Bible believing Christians. Today, only 22 percent belong to a Bible believing church, and over 110 million are unchurched.

In fact, there are over thirty million Americans who are militantly anti-Christian.

The inroads of humanism, liberalism, and anti-God belief in America are frightening. If present trends continue, by the year 2025 the United States of America will be the center of atheism and unbelief and one of the largest spiritually unreached countries in the world!

But some would ask, "church planting here in America? Shouldn't we spend our time and money reaching the heathen?" The facts are: an increasing secularization and a growing immigrant population make the United States a needy mission field.

There are also those who have the common perception that there are more than enough churches in the United States already. We do well to carefully investigate the facts.

In America, the missionary sending country, we are losing ground. In 1900 there were twenty-eight churches for every 10,000 people. Today there are but nine churches for every 10,000 people in the United States. The number of churched people in the good old USA is rapidly declining.

In many of the 350,000 churches in America, the gospel is not preached, nor is biblical doctrine taught. One leading church growth expert recently stated, "In the past twenty years, our emphasis and church growth principles have made little change in the spiritual vitality of America. All we have done is to transfer people from the smaller churches to the megachurches."

To evangelize, and then disciple this growing body of unbelievers, we need a multitude of missionaries who will plant Christ centered, Bible believing churches.

And the people who are members of Bible believing churches need to be instilled with a vision for mission-field America. May our Lord lay this mission field heavy upon your heart and mine. May God open our eyes and our hearts to "see the world, Lord, as though I were looking through Your eyes."

The fact is, if we do not catch a vision for church planting in America, there will also be a dwindling base for mission outreach worldwide.

Church planting in the United States is an investment in world missions. Each church planted represents future missionaries, more people praying for world missions, and a broadening financial base for world missions.

The bottom line is this—the primary reason for planting churches in America is that there are unsaved people, perhaps people living next door to you or me, who need to hear the good news of salvation by grace through faith.

Our investment of life, time, and finances in church planting is an investment in the eternal souls of men, women, boys, and girls—indeed, an investment for eternity!

May we have a clear and empowering vision of what Christ would do through us to reach mission-field America!

We Christians are called to be agents of change in a sinful world. It is the commitment of NICE to work toward that change through planting and establishing churches. In his book, *The Vanishing Ministry*, Woodrow Kroll says it well: "There is an obvious and immediate result to planting churches in America. If the new church is built on new converts, and not just disgruntled church hoppers, there will be a wave of evangelism sweep the USA as a wave of churches are planted. Men and women will trust Christ as saviour. Homes will be put back together. Families will be strengthened. Moral and spiritual values will be changed. America will be better off."

The time is now! The time for church planting! The time to make a difference for the outreach of the gospel. We may not have tomorrow!

Chapter 16

Vision For Tomorrow

As we move into the twenty-first century, we must not only have vision for the days ahead, but we also must have a strong commitment to a strategy that will facilitate the fulfillment of our vision.

With this in view, the board of directors of the mission have adopted the following:

Statement of Vision:

> We envision NICE as a fellowship of committed servants of Jesus Christ, aggressively involved in planting, establishing, and serving churches among all people groups, prayerfully working together with our constituent churches in a spirit of interdependence.

Statement of Strategy:

In fulfilling our purpose and vision, we are committed to excellence in the pursuit of the following goals:

1. Our *focus* is to make disciples of Jesus Christ.

We will challenge, teach, train, and equip God's servants to not only win the lost, but also to root and ground the new believers in the Word of God and to train leaders to become spiritual reproducers.

We will plan and schedule seminars and conferences in the churches, that will emphasize evangelism and disciple making.

We will develop evangelism and discipleship resources for use by our missionaries and churches.

We will emphasize the importance of making disciples through our publications.

We will use the Mobile Chapel as a challenge toward evangelism.

2. Our *method* is to plant, establish and serve churches.

We will emphasize the necessity of planting churches wherever and whenever possible.

We will recruit church planters and missionary pastors for these ministries by contacts with schools and churches and through the internet.

We will teach and train church planters through our school of ministry and other avenues available.

We will work with the church planters and missionary pastors to assist them in establishing the churches planted and served.

3. Our *desire* is to reach the next city or town where there is no doctrinally sound fundamental church.

We will carefully monitor the trends in population growth.

We will systematically survey cities and towns to determine the spiritual needs.

We will target by prayer and publication those cities and towns that especially need a church.

We will focus on these targeted locations until the planting of a church is accomplished and the spiritual need met.

We will initiate special projects to secure funds to implement planting churches in these high priority locations.

4.   Our *priority* is ministry to people, not programs, land, or buildings.

We will demonstrate that people are our priority by the example of servant leadership to our missionaries, their families, and to the churches.

We will demonstrate that people are our priority by expressing our deep appreciation for our missionaries, our supporters, and our prayer partners.

We will demonstrate that people are our priority by continuing to strengthen our relationships with people, and to focus on people in the *NICE Digest*, *The Increase*, and the praise and prayer booklets.

5.   Our *emphasis* is evangelism of the lost, not taking away members from existing Bible believing churches.

We will emphasize in all of our ministry the need of salvation by grace through faith.

We will be available for evangelism training, and evangelistic meetings.

We will promote evangelism by encouraging our missionaries to reach out to all unsaved people, wherever the Lord opens the door.

We will dedicate issues of *The Increase* to evangelism, and will produce materials which encourage evangelism.

We will coordinate with the IFCA regional in planning
conferences, which focus on evangelism and feature tools
of evangelism for our churches and leaders.

6. Our *love* will seek to reach people in their own language and culture.

We will actively promote the need for ethnic church
planting ministries in our constituent churches.
We will carefully monitor the trends in ethnic population growth.
We will target by prayer and publication those cities and
towns which especially need a fundamental ethnic church.
We will seek to recruit ethnic church planters for the
various ethnic communities of the Northwest.
We will not neglect making efforts to reach any ethnic
group, including those which are primarily anglo.

7. Our *ministry* will use a variety of methods to plant and establish churches.

We will use various avenues of evangelism in church
planting and growth.
We will use home Bible classes as a means of church
planting and growth.
We will use visitation to provide contacts for church
planting and growth.
We will use youth and children's ministries as a means
of church planting and growth.
We will use special meetings to provide contacts for
church planting and growth.
We will use advertising, direct mail, the telephone, and
the internet to provide contacts for church planting and
growth.

8. Our *involvement* will include a sponsoring church or churches when possible.

> We will challenge churches to plant daughter churches
> We will encourage churches to adopt a mission church.
> We will urge individuals to adopt a NICE missionary.

9. Our *concern* will be to edify and equip believers for ministry.

> We will develop Bible study resources and make them available to our missionaries and churches.
> We will refine our missionary in-training and pastoral mentoring program.
> We will work with the IFCA regionals and churches in the expansion of the pastoral mentoring program.

10. Our *dedication* is to scriptural and ethical practices in every matter.

> We will urge individuals and churches toward biblical living and practice.
> We will seek to emphasize and model integrity in all of our ministry.
> We will follow biblical principles and patterns in all matters of individual life, church life, and church government.
> We will review mission policies regularly, so as always to be current in relation to ethical issues.
> We will follow biblical principles and patterns in all matters of conflict resolution and discipline.
> We will provide seminars and conferences, which will train leaders in scriptural and ethical practices.

11. Our *workers* shall be committed to our biblical convictions.

We will regularly evaluate our recruiting and application procedures.

We will expect an annual recommitment from all mission workers and churches.

We will provide seminars and conferences, which will address the biblical basis for our convictions and doctrinal position.

12. Our *leadership* will strive for godliness and moral purity.

We will covenant to build up and strengthen one another by prayer, study of the Word, and mutual accountability.

We will urge NICE personnel not to become involved in long term counseling of those of the opposite sex.

We will urge all personnel to never let down their guard and to remember that special temptation may follow victory.

We will seek to schedule conferences and seminars, which will address the matter of moral purity.

13. Our *wish* is for each church planted or served to associate with IFCA International.

We will encourage IFCA membership by declaring the benefits of our fellowship through our publications.

We will make IFCA membership packets available whenever and wherever possible.

We will urge the churches served to join IFCA International.

We will expect our missionaries to attend their IFCA regional conferences as often as possible.

14. Our *commitment* is to prayer, recognizing that the work of God is spiritual warfare.

We will encourage prayer for one another through the *NICE Digest*, the praise and prayer reports, and the missionary prayer letters.
We will pray for mission personnel and churches at the start of each day in the mission office.
We will meet annually for days of prayer at which time the mission leadership will concertedly pray for people and ministries.

15. Our *eyes* will be upon Him, for He is the Lord of the Church.

We covenant to commit every aspect of life and ministry to the Lord, always seeking His mind and His direction.
We acknowledge that this ministry belongs to Him!

Statement of Victory

The ultimate victory is yet to be, when we stand before the throne of God and see "a great multitude, which no man could number, of all nations, and kindreds, and peoples, and tongues, standing before the throne, and before the Lamb ... saying, Salvation to our God who sitteth upon the throne, and to the Lamb" (Rev. 7:9–10).

What a day that will be! Praise God for many, many precious souls in glory because of the ministry of Northwest Independent Church Extension.

Faith Bible Church of Fernley, Founded 1981

Carson Bible Church, Founded 1972

They're NICE!

Board of Directors (Year indicates when ministry with NICE began):
1958
   Mr. W. Henry Boyd
   Rev. Charles Lyman
   Rev. Noel E. Olsen
   Rev. Richard Schwab
   Dr. Wallace R. Wilson
1959
   Mr. William Denney
   Mr. Joseph Kempston
1962
   Mr. Leland L. Lowry
1963
   Rev. Calvin Harrah
1964
   Rev. Glenn E. Davis
   Rev. Arnold Wall
1965
   Rev. Virgil Vater

1966
Rev. Bernard LeRoy
Mr. Wayne Stewart
1967
Dr. Daniel Sauerwein
1968
Mr. Maco Allason
1971
Rev. William E. Cross
Rev. Roland Frederick
1972
Rev. Jack M. Perry
Mr. John Stenger
1973
Rev. Leroy Jackson
1975
Rev. William Flemming
1976
Rev. Ron E. Eggert
1977
Dr. D. Michael Jones
Rev. Terry Parks
1978
Mr. John A. Smith
1980
Rev. Charles Allison
1981
Rev. John A. Edgell
1982
Rev. Ralph Anderegg
1984
Rev. Timothy G. Walton

1985
Rev. Neil Beery
1986
Dr. Robert Ohlson
Dr. Lowell C. Wendt
1987
Rev. Ernest Quaintance
Rev. Stan Scholl
1989
Rev. Garland R. Shinn
1990
Dr. Jack Teachout
1994
Rev. Donn Jackson
Rev. George Williams
1995
Mr. Alvin Kessler
1996
Rev. Gerald D. James
1998
Dr. Rodric Pence

Missionaries:
1958
Mr. and Mrs. W. Henry Boyd
Rev. and Mrs. Donald Martin
Rev. and Mrs. Ed Snyder
1959
Rev. and Mrs. Gene Almquist
Miss Marie Brown
Rev. and Mrs. Donald Strunk
Rev. and Mrs. Gordon Titus
Rev. and Mrs. Charles Witcher

1960

Rev. and Mrs. Roy Rhodes

Dr. and Mrs. Roy E. Sprague

Mr. and Mrs. Cass Vincent

1961

Rev. and Mrs. James Hendricks

Rev. and Mrs. Wesley Mansfield

1962

Mr. Frank Mecklenburg

Mr. and Mrs. Dean Smith

1965

Rev. and Mrs. Earl Brubaker

Mr. and Mrs. Frank Furnish

Rev. and Mrs. Robert Haskell

Rev. and Mrs. W. Homer Poland

1966

Rev. Fred Curow

Rev. and Mrs. Donald Greenwood

Rev. and Mrs. Jim Johnson

Rev. Carey Smith

1967

Rev. and Mrs. Leslie Ensley

Rev. and Mrs. Richard Grover

Rev. and Mrs. Gerald D. James

Rev. and Mrs. Neal Matthews

1968

Rev. and Mrs. Evert Atkinson

Rev. and Mrs. Willis Baker

Rev. and Mrs. Jerry Coon

Rev. and Mrs. Glenn Kirsch

Rev. and Mrs. Donald Wantland

1969

Mr. and Mrs. Curt Fox
Rev. and Mrs. Bill Geyer
Mr. and Mrs. Barry Sell
Rev. and Mrs. Clyde West

1970

Mr. and Mrs. Dean Brainard
Mr. and Mrs. David Kerns
Dr. and Mrs. Dwight Paulson
Mr. and Mrs. Howard Stocks

1971

Miss Joann Coffield
Mr. and Mrs. Winston Newton

1972

Rev. and Mrs. Claude Brown
Rev. and Mrs. Charles Butler
Rev. and Mrs. Charles Hill
Mr. and Mrs. Stuart Garbutt
Mr. and Mrs. John Karling
Mr. Philip Kirsch
Rev. and Mrs. Monty Martin
Rev. and Mrs. Timothy Walton

1973

Rev. and Mrs. Timothy Baker
Mr. and Mrs. Stephen Doty
Rev. and Mrs. Robert Lowry
Rev. and Mrs. Myrl Root

1974

Rev. and Mrs. John Edgell
Rev. and Mrs. Lloyd Hawkins
Mr. and Mrs. Roger Johnson
Rev. and Mrs. Clarence Nase

1974

Rev. and Mrs. Vincent Ortiz

Mr. and Mrs. Timothy Schwartz

1975

Rev. and Mrs. Kenneth Chism

Rev. and Mrs. Edward Graham

Rev. and Mrs. James Nash

Dr. and Mrs. Robert Ohlson

Rev. and Mrs. Garland Shinn

Rev. and Mrs. W.D. Ward

Rev. and Mrs. Dan Wentworth

1976

Mr. and Mrs. Frank Colletto

Mr. and Mrs. Eston Gillett

Rev. and Mrs. Gregory Griffith

Rev. and Mrs. Jim Jamieson

Mr. Jack Kessler

Mr. Tom Pousche

Rev. and Mrs. Thomas Randall

Mr. and Mrs. Jim Schlaegel

Rev. and Mrs. Jonathan Smith

Mr. Neale Sorrels

Mr. and Mrs. Craig Swineford

Rev. and Mrs. Mark Warrington

1977

Rev. and Mrs. Arthur Bauer

Rev. and Mrs. Richard Casad

Rev. and Mrs. Steven Francis

Rev. and Mrs. Randall Fulton

Mr. and Mrs. Eugene Greyn

Mr. and Mrs. Thomas Hayden

Rev. and Mrs. Charles Holgate

1977

Mr. and Mrs. Richard Lewis
Mr. David Medalen
Mr. and Mrs. Daryl Miller
Rev. and Mrs. James Miller
Mr. and Mrs. Vance Shafer
Rev. and Mrs. Don D. Srail
Mr. and Mrs. Meredith Wheeler
Mr. and Mrs. Leland Whitlatch

1978

Rev. and Mrs. Jerry Adams
Rev. and Mrs. John Reed
Rev. and Mrs. Bruce Root

1979

Dr. Edison G. Cheek, Jr.
Rev. and Mrs. Morrison Fisher
Rev. and Mrs. Anders Lundin
Rev. and Mrs. Robert Morris
Mr. and Mrs. Claude Vandevert

1980

Mr. and Mrs. Jack Clapp
Rev. and Mrs. Kenneth Davis
Rev. and Mrs. Stan Poeschel
Rev. and Mrs. Andrew Simonson
Mr. Harold Turpin
Mr. George Washington, Jr.
Mr. and Mrs. Ed Wiley
Rev. and Mrs. Ray Woolford

1981

Rev. and Mrs. Terry Berreth
Rev. and Mrs. Larry Carlson
Mr. and Mrs. Robert Dillard
Rev. and Mrs. Douglas Garland

1981

Rev. Rex Heckel
Rev. and Mrs. David Martin
Rev. and Mrs. Jonathan Teeter

1982

Rev. and Mrs. Prentice Boyd
Rev. and Mrs. James Downing
Rev. and Mrs. Frank Emrich
Mr. and Mrs. Willard English
Mr. and Mrs. John Ginther
Rev. and Mrs. Robert Rodgers

1983

Rev. and Mrs. Harlan Benthien
Rev. and Mrs. Norval Brown
Mr. and Mrs. James Coffman
Rev. and Mrs. James Cornell
Mr. and Mrs. David Fooks
Mr. and Mrs. Roger Gillihan
Rev. and Mrs. Earl Hinkle
Rev. and Mrs. Dennis Kreiss
Rev. and Mrs. Craig Lawless
Rev. and Mrs. Keith Lyons
Rev. and Mrs. Duane Marvin
Rev. and Mrs. Bill West

1984

Rev. and Mrs. Jerry Hill
Rev. and Mrs. Larry Ott
Rev. and Mrs. Bill Stoliker

1985

Rev. and Mrs. Bill Peters
Rev. and Mrs. Lloyd Russell
Rev. and Mrs. Nathan Shinn

1985

Rev. and Mrs. Timothy Tontz
Rev. and Mrs. Randy Turner

1986

Rev. and Mrs. Thomas Brown
Rev. and Mrs. Douglas Cartwright
Rev. and Mrs. Thomas Drenoske
Rev. and Mrs. Jerry Ingram
Rev. and Mrs. Mark LaFortune
Mr. and Mrs. Thomas Lawson
Rev. and Mrs. Ernest Quaintance
Mr. and Mrs. Thomas Schwartz
Rev. and Mrs. David Yost

1987

Mr. and Mrs. Hugh Adams
Dr. and Mrs. Alan Niquette
Rev. and Mrs. Mark Simpson

1988

Mr. and Mrs. Clayton Ciolek
Dr. and Mrs. Bill Lyons
Mr. Dan Marvin
Mr. and Mrs. John Pollard
Rev. and Mrs. John Teeter

1989

Dr. and Mrs. Jerry Back
Rev. and Mrs. Peter Banks
Rev. and Mrs. Darrell Fraley
Rev. and Mrs. John McDaniel
Mr. and Mrs. Mike Philipsen
Mr. Rick Wood

1990

Rev. and Mrs. Jerry Conklin
Rev. and Mrs. Steve DeFord
Mr. and Mrs. Martin McDowell
Mr. and Mrs. Edward O'Leary
Mr. and Mrs. Mark Pryor
Mr. and Mrs. Terry Strunk

1991

Rev. and Mrs. Jonathan Beyer
Mr. and Mrs. Steve Braun
Rev. and Mrs. Fred DeVos
Rev. and Mrs. Kelley McCormick
Rev. and Mrs. Jeff Mullins
Mr. and Mrs. Robert Thompson

1992

Mr. and Mrs. Robert Allen
Mr. and Mrs. Michael Lutz
Rev. and Mrs. Samuel Perkins
Rev. and Mrs. Zane Richardson
Rev. and Mrs. David Singleton
Mr. and Mrs. John A. Smith

1993

Mr. and Mrs. James Hiatt
Rev. and Mrs. Rodney Jones
Mr. Carsten Plewka

1994

Rev. and Mrs. Richard Bingham
Rev. and Mrs. Jesús Cordova
Rev. and Mrs. Roger Hayden
Rev. and Mrs. Chris McGreer
Rev. and Mrs. Jon Vietti

1995

Rev. and Mrs. Dale Valovich
Mr. and Mrs. John Wagner
Dr. and Mrs. Joel Wallace

1996

Mr. and Mrs. Jerry Poeschel

1997

Mr. and Mrs. James Edgell
Rev. and Mrs. Joseph Kontz

1998

Rev. and Mrs. Robert Archer
Rev. and Mrs. George Riffle
Rev. and Mrs. Matthew Sconce

Nathan and Muriel Shinn
and family

Sam and Joy Perkins and family

Roger and Karen Hayden

Steve and Celeste Deford and family

Immanuel Baptist Church, Klamath Falls, Oregon

Mobile chapel in memory of Rev. and Mrs. Harry A. Sprague

Lewis and Clark Bible Church, Astoria, Oregon

Wishkah Valley Community Church, Aberdeen, Washington

Richard and Kristen Bingham and family

Bob and Katherine Rodgers and family

Can NICE Serve You?

If you believe that God wants to use you in a Church planting ministry serving with NICE, please contact the Mission Office.

If you believe that God wants to use you to plant a Church in your area, we stand ready to help in every way possible to see a Bible-believing Church planted; please contact the Mission Office.

If you would like to receive further information concerning NICE's purpose, its ministry, and its policies, please contact the Mission Office today!

Northwest Independent Church Extension
PO Box 99787 Tacoma, WA 98499-0787
Voice: (253) 564-NICE
Fax: (253) 565-6194
E-mail: NICE@ifca.org

To order additional copies of:

From Vision to Venture to Victory

send $9.95 plus $3.95 shipping and handling to:

Books, Etc.
PO Box 1406
Mukilteo, WA 98275

or have your credit card ready and call:

(800) 917-BOOK